LOVE

IN PROGRESS

SET IN SOUL

DEDICATED TO THOSE COMMITTED TO LOVING EACH OTHER

THIS JOURNAL BELONGS TO

_____

TABLE OF CONTENTS

HOW TO USE THIS JOURNAL

Let's have some fun. Boy meets girl and girl says...Well this is for you to fill out as a couple. It's time for you to write and record your story. What better way to do that then to have a book all about your love. The good. The bad. The surprising. Write it down. This journal is not only a record of what you two have done thus far, but also a record of where you are going. Write down your goals as a couple, and keep track of your goals by being each other's daily accountability partner. Everyday, learn what he wants from you. Everyday, learn what she wants from you. Write down your love messages of the day and grow closer in communication.

It is recommended that you write in this journal daily. It is separated by his and her sections, where each of you can see each other's responses to the prompts. When love is needed, friendship is needed, prayer is needed and compassion and patience are needed, this journal serves as a reminder as to what you have, what you have overcome and gives you the strength to get through where you are going - as a couple. This is your chance to be transparent about your love story. As you embark on your love journey together, you will realize that through the highs and the lows, you are truly creating a union that has been brought together for a purpose that serves you both. This is your Love In Progress.

ABOUT US

His Full Name:

THOMAS ALAN SHULL

Her Full Name:

Our Ages:

58

We Met On This Date:

199

We Met At This Place: COUNTY ADMIN BUILDING

Our First Kiss:

ABOUT US

Our First Date:

Our First Conversation On The Phone Lasted:

The First Thing We Bought Together:

Our First Vacation:

BONAIRE

Our First Anniversary, We Spent It:

Our First Dance Happened:

ABOUT US

First Time We Said I Love You:

Our First Disagreement Was About:

Our Favorite Breakfast Spot:

Our Favorite Lunch Spot:

Our Favorite Dinner Spot:

ABOUT US

Our Favorite Sports Teams Are:

Our Song:

An Epic Moment We Will Never Forget:

OUR LOVE STORY
(Write It Out)

LOVE PROMPTS
ABOUT HIM
(She Fills This Out About Him)

His Nickname/s For Me:

I Like It When He:

I Love When He Does:

I Always Notice When He:

LOVE PROMPTS ABOUT HIM

One Of My Favorite Scents He Wears:

He Has Helped Me To:

He Says I Remind Him Of:

The Way He Looks At Me Makes Me Feel:

What He Loves About Me:

The First Time He Held My Hand, I:

LOVE PROMPTS ABOUT HIM

The First Time He Cooked For Me:

When I Met His Family, I Felt:

I Knew I Was In Love When:

What He Does And Says That Turns Me On:

A Pet Peeve Of Mine That He Does:

I Can Tell When He Is:

LOVE PROMPTS ABOUT HIM

What I Want Him To Do More Of:

I Like It When He Tells Me:

What I Want Him To Know:

What I Like To Do To Get His Attention:

He Has Always Said This About Me:

Because Of Him I Stopped:

LOVE PROMPTS ABOUT HIM

Because Of Him I Started:

He Makes Me Feel:

What I Would Like Him To Think About Me:

What He Loves About Me That I Did Not Once Love About Myself:

He Likes When I Cook _____For Him.

He Prefers _____Over _____.

I Cherish The _____He Gave Me.

I Can Feel When He Is _____.

I BELIEVE WE WILL:

LOVE PROMPTS
ABOUT HER
(He Fills This Out About Her)

Her Nickname/s For Me:

She Makes Me Laugh When She:

She Makes Me Smile When:

What I Love About Her That Can't Be Replaced:

LOVE PROMPTS ABOUT HER

My Favorite Scent That She Wears:

I Love Doing This For Her:

I Think She Looks Her Best When:

Some Of Her Best Qualities Are:

I Like To Watch Her:

LOVE PROMPTS ABOUT HER

She Taught Me:

Because Of Her I Stopped:

Because Of Her I Started:

She Motivates Me To:

I Can Trust Her With:

LOVE PROMPTS ABOUT HER

When She Looks At Me, I Feel:

I Love When She Does:

The First Time She Cooked For Me:

The First Time I Cooked For Her:

She Gets Angry When I:

LOVE PROMPTS ABOUT HER

She Makes Me Feel:

She Makes Me Want To:

I Love When She:

What I Would Like Her To Think About Me:

What She Says/Does To Turn Me On:

LOVE PROMPTS ABOUT HER

I Knew I Was In Love When:

The Gift I Gave Her That Made Her Smile:

I Always Notice When She:

I'll Always Remember When She Told Me:

She Taught Me To Love _____About Myself.

I Cherish The _____She Gave Me.

I BELIEVE WE WILL:

OUR GOALS TOGETHER

Our Short Term Goals Together:

Our Long Term Goals Together:

What We Are Currently Working On:

Hurdles That We Are Working On Right Now:

LOVE
IN OUR WORDS

Date:

HIS

Today's Goal/s:

What I Want God To Know About Us:

What I Promise Her Today:

What I Want Her To Know Today:

I Am Grateful For Her Because:

It's Important To Me That You:

It's Important To Me That We:

What I Need Today:

What I Did For Myself Today:

HER

Today's Goal/s:

What I Want God To Know About Us:

What I Promise Him Today:

What I Want Him To Know Today:

I Am Grateful For Him Because:

It's Important To Me That You:

It's Important To Me That We:

What I Need Today:

What I Did For Myself Today:

LOVE IN PROGRESS

Date:

HIS | HER

HIS	HER
Today's Goal/s:	Today's Goal/s:
What I Want God To Know About Us:	What I Want God To Know About Us:
What I Promise Her Today:	What I Promise Him Today:
What I Want Her To Know Today:	What I Want Him To Know Today:
I Am Grateful For Her Because:	I Am Grateful For Him Because:
It's Important To Me That You:	It's Important To Me That You:
It's Important To Me That We:	It's Important To Me That We:
What I Need Today:	What I Need Today:
What I Did For Myself Today:	What I Did For Myself Today:

Date:

HIS	HER
Today's Goal/s:	Today's Goal/s:
What I Want God To Know About Us:	What I Want God To Know About Us:
What I Promise Her Today:	What I Promise Him Today:
What I Want Her To Know Today:	What I Want Him To Know Today:
I Am Grateful For Her Because:	I Am Grateful For Him Because:
It's Important To Me That You:	It's Important To Me That You:
It's Important To Me That We:	It's Important To Me That We:
What I Need Today:	What I Need Today:
What I Did For Myself Today:	What I Did For Myself Today:

29

LOVE IN PROGRESS
Date:

HIS

Today's Goal/s:

What I Want God To Know About Us:

What I Promise Her Today:

What I Want Her To Know Today:

I Am Grateful For Her Because:

It's Important To Me That You:

It's Important To Me That We:

What I Need Today:

What I Did For Myself Today:

HER

Today's Goal/s:

What I Want God To Know About Us:

What I Promise Him Today:

What I Want Him To Know Today:

I Am Grateful For Him Because:

It's Important To Me That You:

It's Important To Me That We:

What I Need Today:

What I Did For Myself Today:

Date:

HIS

Today's Goal/s:

What I Want God To Know About Us:

What I Promise Her Today:

What I Want Her To Know Today:

I Am Grateful For Her Because:

It's Important To Me That You:

It's Important To Me That We:

What I Need Today:

What I Did For Myself Today:

HER

Today's Goal/s:

What I Want God To Know About Us:

What I Promise Him Today:

What I Want Him To Know Today:

I Am Grateful For Him Because:

It's Important To Me That You:

It's Important To Me That We:

What I Need Today:

What I Did For Myself Today:

Gentle.
I Am Gentle With Her Heart.

With Everything She Has Given Me,
I Know To Be Gentle. Gentle
With Her Heart.

Date:

HIS

Today's Goal/s:

What I Want God To Know About Us:

What I Promise Her Today:

What I Want Her To Know Today:

I Am Grateful For Her Because:

It's Important To Me That You:

It's Important To Me That We:

What I Need Today:

What I Did For Myself Today:

HER

Today's Goal/s:

What I Want God To Know About Us:

What I Promise Him Today:

What I Want Him To Know Today:

I Am Grateful For Him Because:

It's Important To Me That You:

It's Important To Me That We:

What I Need Today:

What I Did For Myself Today:

Date:

HIS	**HER**
Today's Goal/s:	Today's Goal/s:
What I Want God To Know About Us:	What I Want God To Know About Us:
What I Promise Her Today:	What I Promise Him Today:
What I Want Her To Know Today:	What I Want Him To Know Today:
I Am Grateful For Her Because:	I Am Grateful For Him Because:
It's Important To Me That You:	It's Important To Me That You:
It's Important To Me That We:	It's Important To Me That We:
What I Need Today:	What I Need Today:
What I Did For Myself Today:	What I Did For Myself Today:

OUR MUSIC PLAYLIST TODAY THAT DESCRIBES US

1.

2.

3.

4.

5.

6.

7.

8.

9.

10.

11.

12.

HIS

HER

Today's Goal/s:

Today's Goal/s:

What I Want God To Know About Us:

What I Want God To Know About Us:

What I Promise Her Today:

What I Promise Him Today:

What I Want Her To Know Today:

What I Want Him To Know Today:

I Am Grateful For Her Because:

I Am Grateful For Him Because:

It's Important To Me That You:

It's Important To Me That You:

It's Important To Me That We:

It's Important To Me That We:

What I Need Today:

What I Need Today:

What I Did For Myself Today:

What I Did For Myself Today:

HIS	**HER**
Today's Goal/s:	Today's Goal/s:
What I Want God To Know About Us:	What I Want God To Know About Us:
What I Promise Her Today:	What I Promise Him Today:
What I Want Her To Know Today:	What I Want Him To Know Today:
I Am Grateful For Her Because:	I Am Grateful For Him Because:
It's Important To Me That You:	It's Important To Me That You:
It's Important To Me That We:	It's Important To Me That We:
What I Need Today:	What I Need Today:
What I Did For Myself Today:	What I Did For Myself Today:

HIS	**HER**
Today's Goal/s:	Today's Goal/s:
What I Want God To Know About Us:	What I Want God To Know About Us:
What I Promise Her Today:	What I Promise Him Today:
What I Want Her To Know Today:	What I Want Him To Know Today:
I Am Grateful For Her Because:	I Am Grateful For Him Because:
It's Important To Me That You:	It's Important To Me That You:
It's Important To Me That We:	It's Important To Me That We:
What I Need Today:	What I Need Today:
What I Did For Myself Today:	What I Did For Myself Today:

HIS

Today's Goal/s:

What I Want God To Know About Us:

What I Promise Her Today:

What I Want Her To Know Today:

I Am Grateful For Her Because:

It's Important To Me That You:

It's Important To Me That We:

What I Need Today:

What I Did For Myself Today:

HER

Today's Goal/s:

What I Want God To Know About Us:

What I Promise Him Today:

What I Want Him To Know Today:

I Am Grateful For Him Because:

It's Important To Me That You:

It's Important To Me That We:

What I Need Today:

What I Did For Myself Today:

He

Can Find Love Here.

He Can Find Forgiveness Here. He Will

Date:

HIS	HER
Today's Goal/s:	Today's Goal/s:
What I Want God To Know About Us:	What I Want God To Know About Us:
What I Promise Her Today:	What I Promise Him Today:
What I Want Her To Know Today:	What I Want Him To Know Today:
I Am Grateful For Her Because:	I Am Grateful For Him Because:
It's Important To Me That You:	It's Important To Me That You:
It's Important To Me That We:	It's Important To Me That We:
What I Need Today:	What I Need Today:
What I Did For Myself Today:	What I Did For Myself Today:

LOVE IN PROGRESS
Date:

HIS

Today's Goal/s:

What I Want God To Know About Us:

What I Promise Her Today:

What I Want Her To Know Today:

I Am Grateful For Her Because:

It's Important To Me That You:

It's Important To Me That We:

What I Need Today:

What I Did For Myself Today:

HER

Today's Goal/s:

What I Want God To Know About Us:

What I Promise Him Today:

What I Want Him To Know Today:

I Am Grateful For Him Because:

It's Important To Me That You:

It's Important To Me That We:

What I Need Today:

What I Did For Myself Today:

A PRAYER FOR HIM:

A PRAYER FOR HER:

Date:

HIS

Today's Goal/s:

What I Want God To Know About Us:

What I Promise Her Today:

What I Want Her To Know Today:

I Am Grateful For Her Because:

It's Important To Me That You:

It's Important To Me That We:

What I Need Today:

What I Did For Myself Today:

HER

Today's Goal/s:

What I Want God To Know About Us:

What I Promise Him Today:

What I Want Him To Know Today:

I Am Grateful For Him Because:

It's Important To Me That You:

It's Important To Me That We:

What I Need Today:

What I Did For Myself Today:

Date:

HIS

HER

Today's Goal/s:

What I Want God To Know About Us:

What I Promise Her Today:

What I Want Her To Know Today:

I Am Grateful For Her Because:

It's Important To Me That You:

It's Important To Me That We:

What I Need Today:

What I Did For Myself Today:

Today's Goal/s:

What I Want God To Know About Us:

What I Promise Him Today:

What I Want Him To Know Today:

I Am Grateful For Him Because:

It's Important To Me That You:

It's Important To Me That We:

What I Need Today:

What I Did For Myself Today:

TODAY WE GAINED CLARITY ON

(Discuss Something Both Of You Need Clarity On)

HIS

Today's Goal/s:

What I Want God To Know About Us:

What I Promise Her Today:

What I Want Her To Know Today:

I Am Grateful For Her Because:

It's Important To Me That You:

It's Important To Me That We:

What I Need Today:

What I Did For Myself Today:

HER

Today's Goal/s:

What I Want God To Know About Us:

What I Promise Him Today:

What I Want Him To Know Today:

I Am Grateful For Him Because:

It's Important To Me That You:

It's Important To Me That We:

What I Need Today:

What I Did For Myself Today:

LOVE IN PROGRESS

Date:

HIS	**HER**
Today's Goal/s:	Today's Goal/s:
What I Want God To Know About Us:	What I Want God To Know About Us:
What I Promise Her Today:	What I Promise Him Today:
What I Want Her To Know Today:	What I Want Him To Know Today:
I Am Grateful For Her Because:	I Am Grateful For Him Because:
It's Important To Me That You:	It's Important To Me That You:
It's Important To Me That We:	It's Important To Me That We:
What I Need Today:	What I Need Today:
What I Did For Myself Today:	What I Did For Myself Today:

HIS

Today's Goal/s:

What I Want God To Know About Us:

What I Promise Her Today:

What I Want Her To Know Today:

I Am Grateful For Her Because:

It's Important To Me That You:

It's Important To Me That We:

What I Need Today:

What I Did For Myself Today:

HER

Today's Goal/s:

What I Want God To Know About Us:

What I Promise Him Today:

What I Want Him To Know Today:

I Am Grateful For Him Because:

It's Important To Me That You:

It's Important To Me That We:

What I Need Today:

What I Did For Myself Today:

I'll LOVE

you again and again and again.

I'll say it again and again and again. I will act on love again and again and

Date:

HIS	**HER**
Today's Goal/s:	Today's Goal/s:
What I Want God To Know About Us:	What I Want God To Know About Us:
What I Promise Her Today:	What I Promise Him Today:
What I Want Her To Know Today:	What I Want Him To Know Today:
I Am Grateful For Her Because:	I Am Grateful For Him Because:
It's Important To Me That You:	It's Important To Me That You:
It's Important To Me That We:	It's Important To Me That We:
What I Need Today:	What I Need Today:
What I Did For Myself Today:	What I Did For Myself Today:

HIS	**HER**
Today's Goal/s:	Today's Goal/s:
What I Want God To Know About Us:	What I Want God To Know About Us:
What I Promise Her Today:	What I Promise Him Today:
What I Want Her To Know Today:	What I Want Him To Know Today:
I Am Grateful For Her Because:	I Am Grateful For Him Because:
It's Important To Me That You:	It's Important To Me That You:
It's Important To Me That We:	It's Important To Me That We:
What I Need Today:	What I Need Today:
What I Did For Myself Today:	What I Did For Myself Today:

HE IS:

(Write Down One Word Of What He Is To You)

SHE IS:

(Write Down One Word Of What She Is To You)

LOVE IN PROGRESS
Date:

HIS	**HER**
Today's Goal/s:	Today's Goal/s:
What I Want God To Know About Us:	What I Want God To Know About Us:
What I Promise Her Today:	What I Promise Him Today:
What I Want Her To Know Today:	What I Want Him To Know Today:
I Am Grateful For Her Because:	I Am Grateful For Him Because:
It's Important To Me That You:	It's Important To Me That You:
It's Important To Me That We:	It's Important To Me That We:
What I Need Today:	What I Need Today:
What I Did For Myself Today:	What I Did For Myself Today:

Date:

HIS

Today's Goal/s:

What I Want God To Know About Us:

What I Promise Her Today:

What I Want Her To Know Today:

I Am Grateful For Her Because:

It's Important To Me That You:

It's Important To Me That We:

What I Need Today:

What I Did For Myself Today:

HER

Today's Goal/s:

What I Want God To Know About Us:

What I Promise Him Today:

What I Want Him To Know Today:

I Am Grateful For Him Because:

It's Important To Me That You:

It's Important To Me That We:

What I Need Today:

What I Did For Myself Today:

HIS

HER

Today's Goal/s:

Today's Goal/s:

What I Want God To Know About Us:

What I Want God To Know About Us:

What I Promise Her Today:

What I Promise Him Today:

What I Want Her To Know Today:

What I Want Him To Know Today:

I Am Grateful For Her Because:

I Am Grateful For Him Because:

It's Important To Me That You:

It's Important To Me That You:

It's Important To Me That We:

It's Important To Me That We:

What I Need Today:

What I Need Today:

What I Did For Myself Today:

What I Did For Myself Today:

MY MUSIC PLAYLIST FOR HIM

1.

2.

3.

4.

5.

6.

7.

8.

9.

10.

11.

12.

HIS

HER

HIS	HER
Today's Goal/s:	Today's Goal/s:
What I Want God To Know About Us:	What I Want God To Know About Us:
What I Promise Her Today:	What I Promise Him Today:
What I Want Her To Know Today:	What I Want Him To Know Today:
I Am Grateful For Her Because:	I Am Grateful For Him Because:
It's Important To Me That You:	It's Important To Me That You:
It's Important To Me That We:	It's Important To Me That We:
What I Need Today:	What I Need Today:
What I Did For Myself Today:	What I Did For Myself Today:

Date:

HIS

Today's Goal/s:

What I Want God To Know About Us:

What I Promise Her Today:

What I Want Her To Know Today:

I Am Grateful For Her Because:

It's Important To Me That You:

It's Important To Me That We:

What I Need Today:

What I Did For Myself Today:

HER

Today's Goal/s:

What I Want God To Know About Us:

What I Promise Him Today:

What I Want Him To Know Today:

I Am Grateful For Him Because:

It's Important To Me That You:

It's Important To Me That We:

What I Need Today:

What I Did For Myself Today:

HIS	**HER**
Today's Goal/s:	Today's Goal/s:
What I Want God To Know About Us:	What I Want God To Know About Us:
What I Promise Her Today:	What I Promise Him Today:
What I Want Her To Know Today:	What I Want Him To Know Today:
I Am Grateful For Her Because:	I Am Grateful For Him Because:
It's Important To Me That You:	It's Important To Me That You:
It's Important To Me That We:	It's Important To Me That We:
What I Need Today:	What I Need Today:
What I Did For Myself Today:	What I Did For Myself Today:

Date:

HIS

Today's Goal/s:

What I Want God To Know About Us:

What I Promise Her Today:

What I Want Her To Know Today:

I Am Grateful For Her Because:

It's Important To Me That You:

It's Important To Me That We:

What I Need Today:

What I Did For Myself Today:

HER

Today's Goal/s:

What I Want God To Know About Us:

What I Promise Him Today:

What I Want Him To Know Today:

I Am Grateful For Him Because:

It's Important To Me That You:

It's Important To Me That We:

What I Need Today:

What I Did For Myself Today:

LOVE
Never Fails

— 1 Corinthians 13:8

Date:

HIS

Today's Goal/s:

What I Want God To Know About Us:

What I Promise Her Today:

What I Want Her To Know Today:

I Am Grateful For Her Because:

It's Important To Me That You:

It's Important To Me That We:

What I Need Today:

What I Did For Myself Today:

HER

Today's Goal/s:

What I Want God To Know About Us:

What I Promise Him Today:

What I Want Him To Know Today:

I Am Grateful For Him Because:

It's Important To Me That You:

It's Important To Me That We:

What I Need Today:

What I Did For Myself Today:

HIS   HER

Today's Goal/s: Today's Goal/s:

What I Want God To Know About Us: What I Want God To Know About Us:

What I Promise Her Today: What I Promise Him Today:

What I Want Her To Know Today: What I Want Him To Know Today:

I Am Grateful For Her Because: I Am Grateful For Him Because:

It's Important To Me That You: It's Important To Me That You:

It's Important To Me That We: It's Important To Me That We:

What I Need Today: What I Need Today:

What I Did For Myself Today: What I Did For Myself Today:

Date:

HIS

Today's Goal/s:

What I Want God To Know About Us:

What I Promise Her Today:

What I Want Her To Know Today:

I Am Grateful For Her Because:

It's Important To Me That You:

It's Important To Me That We:

What I Need Today:

What I Did For Myself Today:

HER

Today's Goal/s:

What I Want God To Know About Us:

What I Promise Him Today:

What I Want Him To Know Today:

I Am Grateful For Him Because:

It's Important To Me That You:

It's Important To Me That We:

What I Need Today:

What I Did For Myself Today:

HIS

HER

HIS	HER
Today's Goal/s:	Today's Goal/s:
What I Want God To Know About Us:	What I Want God To Know About Us:
What I Promise Her Today:	What I Promise Him Today:
What I Want Her To Know Today:	What I Want Him To Know Today:
I Am Grateful For Her Because:	I Am Grateful For Him Because:
It's Important To Me That You:	It's Important To Me That You:
It's Important To Me That We:	It's Important To Me That We:
What I Need Today:	What I Need Today:
What I Did For Myself Today:	What I Did For Myself Today:

TODAY WE GAINED CLARITY ON

(Discuss Something Both Of You Need Clarity On)

LOVE IN PROGRESS

Date:

HIS	HER
Today's Goal/s:	Today's Goal/s:
What I Want God To Know About Us:	What I Want God To Know About Us:
What I Promise Her Today:	What I Promise Him Today:
What I Want Her To Know Today:	What I Want Him To Know Today:
I Am Grateful For Her Because:	I Am Grateful For Him Because:
It's Important To Me That You:	It's Important To Me That You:
It's Important To Me That We:	It's Important To Me That We:
What I Need Today:	What I Need Today:
What I Did For Myself Today:	What I Did For Myself Today:

Date:

HIS

Today's Goal/s:

What I Want God To Know About Us:

What I Promise Her Today:

What I Want Her To Know Today:

I Am Grateful For Her Because:

It's Important To Me That You:

It's Important To Me That We:

What I Need Today:

What I Did For Myself Today:

HER

Today's Goal/s:

What I Want God To Know About Us:

What I Promise Him Today:

What I Want Him To Know Today:

I Am Grateful For Him Because:

It's Important To Me That You:

It's Important To Me That We:

What I Need Today:

What I Did For Myself Today:

Date:

HIS

Today's Goal/s:

What I Want God To Know About Us:

What I Promise Her Today:

What I Want Her To Know Today:

I Am Grateful For Her Because:

It's Important To Me That You:

It's Important To Me That We:

What I Need Today:

What I Did For Myself Today:

HER

Today's Goal/s:

What I Want God To Know About Us:

What I Promise Him Today:

What I Want Him To Know Today:

I Am Grateful For Him Because:

It's Important To Me That You:

It's Important To Me That We:

What I Need Today:

What I Did For Myself Today:

LOVE IN PROGRESS

Date:

HIS	**HER**
Today's Goal/s:	Today's Goal/s:
What I Want God To Know About Us:	What I Want God To Know About Us:
What I Promise Her Today:	What I Promise Him Today:
What I Want Her To Know Today:	What I Want Him To Know Today:
I Am Grateful For Her Because:	I Am Grateful For Him Because:
It's Important To Me That You:	It's Important To Me That You:
It's Important To Me That We:	It's Important To Me That We:
What I Need Today:	What I Need Today:
What I Did For Myself Today:	What I Did For Myself Today:

I've

Got Your Back.

You Must Know This.

Date:

HIS

Today's Goal/s:

What I Want God To Know About Us:

What I Promise Her Today:

What I Want Her To Know Today:

I Am Grateful For Her Because:

It's Important To Me That You:

It's Important To Me That We:

What I Need Today:

What I Did For Myself Today:

HER

Today's Goal/s:

What I Want God To Know About Us:

What I Promise Him Today:

What I Want Him To Know Today:

I Am Grateful For Him Because:

It's Important To Me That You:

It's Important To Me That We:

What I Need Today:

What I Did For Myself Today:

HIS

Today's Goal/s:

What I Want God To Know About Us:

What I Promise Her Today:

What I Want Her To Know Today:

I Am Grateful For Her Because:

It's Important To Me That You:

It's Important To Me That We:

What I Need Today:

What I Did For Myself Today:

HER

Today's Goal/s:

What I Want God To Know About Us:

What I Promise Him Today:

What I Want Him To Know Today:

I Am Grateful For Him Because:

It's Important To Me That You:

It's Important To Me That We:

What I Need Today:

What I Did For Myself Today:

HIS

Today's Goal/s:

What I Want God To Know About Us:

What I Promise Her Today:

What I Want Her To Know Today:

I Am Grateful For Her Because:

It's Important To Me That You:

It's Important To Me That We:

What I Need Today:

What I Did For Myself Today:

HER

Today's Goal/s:

What I Want God To Know About Us:

What I Promise Him Today:

What I Want Him To Know Today:

I Am Grateful For Him Because:

It's Important To Me That You:

It's Important To Me That We:

What I Need Today:

What I Did For Myself Today:

HIS

Today's Goal/s:

What I Want God To Know About Us:

What I Promise Her Today:

What I Want Her To Know Today:

I Am Grateful For Her Because:

It's Important To Me That You:

It's Important To Me That We:

What I Need Today:

What I Did For Myself Today:

HER

Today's Goal/s:

What I Want God To Know About Us:

What I Promise Him Today:

What I Want Him To Know Today:

I Am Grateful For Him Because:

It's Important To Me That You:

It's Important To Me That We:

What I Need Today:

What I Did For Myself Today:

HIS RESPONSE:

(What Can I Do To Show You How Much I Love You?)

HER RESPONSE:

(What Can I Do To Show You How Much I Love You?)

LOVE IN PROGRESS

Date:

HIS	**HER**
Today's Goal/s:	Today's Goal/s:
What I Want God To Know About Us:	What I Want God To Know About Us:
What I Promise Her Today:	What I Promise Him Today:
What I Want Her To Know Today:	What I Want Him To Know Today:
I Am Grateful For Her Because:	I Am Grateful For Him Because:
It's Important To Me That You:	It's Important To Me That You:
It's Important To Me That We:	It's Important To Me That We:
What I Need Today:	What I Need Today:
What I Did For Myself Today:	What I Did For Myself Today:

Date:

HIS

Today's Goal/s:

What I Want God To Know About Us:

What I Promise Her Today:

What I Want Her To Know Today:

I Am Grateful For Her Because:

It's Important To Me That You:

It's Important To Me That We:

What I Need Today:

What I Did For Myself Today:

HER

Today's Goal/s:

What I Want God To Know About Us:

What I Promise Him Today:

What I Want Him To Know Today:

I Am Grateful For Him Because:

It's Important To Me That You:

It's Important To Me That We:

What I Need Today:

What I Did For Myself Today:

MY MUSIC PLAYLIST FOR HER

1.

2.

3.

4.

5.

6.

7.

8.

9.

10.

11.

12.

Date:

HIS	HER
Today's Goal/s:	Today's Goal/s:
What I Want God To Know About Us:	What I Want God To Know About Us:
What I Promise Her Today:	What I Promise Him Today:
What I Want Her To Know Today:	What I Want Him To Know Today:
I Am Grateful For Her Because:	I Am Grateful For Him Because:
It's Important To Me That You:	It's Important To Me That You:
It's Important To Me That We:	It's Important To Me That We:
What I Need Today:	What I Need Today:
What I Did For Myself Today:	What I Did For Myself Today:

LOVE IN PROGRESS
Date:

HIS	**HER**
Today's Goal/s:	Today's Goal/s:
What I Want God To Know About Us:	What I Want God To Know About Us:
What I Promise Her Today:	What I Promise Him Today:
What I Want Her To Know Today:	What I Want Him To Know Today:
I Am Grateful For Her Because:	I Am Grateful For Him Because:
It's Important To Me That You:	It's Important To Me That You:
It's Important To Me That We:	It's Important To Me That We:
What I Need Today:	What I Need Today:
What I Did For Myself Today:	What I Did For Myself Today:

Date:

HIS

Today's Goal/s:

What I Want God To Know About Us:

What I Promise Her Today:

What I Want Her To Know Today:

I Am Grateful For Her Because:

It's Important To Me That You:

It's Important To Me That We:

What I Need Today:

What I Did For Myself Today:

HER

Today's Goal/s:

What I Want God To Know About Us:

What I Promise Him Today:

What I Want Him To Know Today:

I Am Grateful For Him Because:

It's Important To Me That You:

It's Important To Me That We:

What I Need Today:

What I Did For Myself Today:

VENI
VIDI
AMAVI

We Came. We Saw. We Loved.

Date:

HIS

Today's Goal/s:

What I Want God To Know About Us:

What I Promise Her Today:

What I Want Her To Know Today:

I Am Grateful For Her Because:

It's Important To Me That You:

It's Important To Me That We:

What I Need Today:

What I Did For Myself Today:

HER

Today's Goal/s:

What I Want God To Know About Us:

What I Promise Him Today:

What I Want Him To Know Today:

I Am Grateful For Him Because:

It's Important To Me That You:

It's Important To Me That We:

What I Need Today:

What I Did For Myself Today:

HIS

Today's Goal/s:

What I Want God To Know About Us:

What I Promise Her Today:

What I Want Her To Know Today:

I Am Grateful For Her Because:

It's Important To Me That You:

It's Important To Me That We:

What I Need Today:

What I Did For Myself Today:

HER

Today's Goal/s:

What I Want God To Know About Us:

What I Promise Him Today:

What I Want Him To Know Today:

I Am Grateful For Him Because:

It's Important To Me That You:

It's Important To Me That We:

What I Need Today:

What I Did For Myself Today:

TODAY'S MAIN QUESTION FOR HER:

HER ANSWER:

HIS

Today's Goal/s:

What I Want God To Know About Us:

What I Promise Her Today:

What I Want Her To Know Today:

I Am Grateful For Her Because:

It's Important To Me That You:

It's Important To Me That We:

What I Need Today:

What I Did For Myself Today:

HER

Today's Goal/s:

What I Want God To Know About Us:

What I Promise Him Today:

What I Want Him To Know Today:

I Am Grateful For Him Because:

It's Important To Me That You:

It's Important To Me That We:

What I Need Today:

What I Did For Myself Today:

Date:

HIS

Today's Goal/s:

What I Want God To Know About Us:

What I Promise Her Today:

What I Want Her To Know Today:

I Am Grateful For Her Because:

It's Important To Me That You:

It's Important To Me That We:

What I Need Today:

What I Did For Myself Today:

HER

Today's Goal/s:

What I Want God To Know About Us:

What I Promise Him Today:

What I Want Him To Know Today:

I Am Grateful For Him Because:

It's Important To Me That You:

It's Important To Me That We:

What I Need Today:

What I Did For Myself Today:

Date:

HIS

Today's Goal/s:

What I Want God To Know About Us:

What I Promise Her Today:

What I Want Her To Know Today:

I Am Grateful For Her Because:

It's Important To Me That You:

It's Important To Me That We:

What I Need Today:

What I Did For Myself Today:

HER

Today's Goal/s:

What I Want God To Know About Us:

What I Promise Him Today:

What I Want Him To Know Today:

I Am Grateful For Him Because:

It's Important To Me That You:

It's Important To Me That We:

What I Need Today:

What I Did For Myself Today:

Date:

HIS

Today's Goal/s:

What I Want God To Know About Us:

What I Promise Her Today:

What I Want Her To Know Today:

I Am Grateful For Her Because:

It's Important To Me That You:

It's Important To Me That We:

What I Need Today:

What I Did For Myself Today:

HER

Today's Goal/s:

What I Want God To Know About Us:

What I Promise Him Today:

What I Want Him To Know Today:

I Am Grateful For Him Because:

It's Important To Me That You:

It's Important To Me That We:

What I Need Today:

What I Did For Myself Today:

Date:

HIS | HER

Today's Goal/s:

What I Want God To Know About Us:

What I Promise Her Today:

What I Want Her To Know Today:

I Am Grateful For Her Because:

It's Important To Me That You:

It's Important To Me That We:

What I Need Today:

What I Did For Myself Today:

Today's Goal/s:

What I Want God To Know About Us:

What I Promise Him Today:

What I Want Him To Know Today:

I Am Grateful For Him Because:

It's Important To Me That You:

It's Important To Me That We:

What I Need Today:

What I Did For Myself Today:

HIS	**HER**
Today's Goal/s:	Today's Goal/s:
What I Want God To Know About Us:	What I Want God To Know About Us:
What I Promise Her Today:	What I Promise Him Today:
What I Want Her To Know Today:	What I Want Him To Know Today:
I Am Grateful For Her Because:	I Am Grateful For Him Because:
It's Important To Me That You:	It's Important To Me That You:
It's Important To Me That We:	It's Important To Me That We:
What I Need Today:	What I Need Today:
What I Did For Myself Today:	What I Did For Myself Today:

MY
L O V E

My Trust. My Best Friend.

Date:

HIS

Today's Goal/s:

What I Want God To Know About Us:

What I Promise Her Today:

What I Want Her To Know Today:

I Am Grateful For Her Because:

It's Important To Me That You:

It's Important To Me That We:

What I Need Today:

What I Did For Myself Today:

HER

Today's Goal/s:

What I Want God To Know About Us:

What I Promise Him Today:

What I Want Him To Know Today:

I Am Grateful For Him Because:

It's Important To Me That You:

It's Important To Me That We:

What I Need Today:

What I Did For Myself Today:

Date:

HIS	HER
Today's Goal/s:	Today's Goal/s:
What I Want God To Know About Us:	What I Want God To Know About Us:
What I Promise Her Today:	What I Promise Him Today:
What I Want Her To Know Today:	What I Want Him To Know Today:
I Am Grateful For Her Because:	I Am Grateful For Him Because:
It's Important To Me That You:	It's Important To Me That You:
It's Important To Me That We:	It's Important To Me That We:
What I Need Today:	What I Need Today:
What I Did For Myself Today:	What I Did For Myself Today:

Date:

HIS

HER

Today's Goal/s:

Today's Goal/s:

What I Want God To Know About Us:

What I Want God To Know About Us:

What I Promise Her Today:

What I Promise Him Today:

What I Want Her To Know Today:

What I Want Him To Know Today:

I Am Grateful For Her Because:

I Am Grateful For Him Because:

It's Important To Me That You:

It's Important To Me That You:

It's Important To Me That We:

It's Important To Me That We:

What I Need Today:

What I Need Today:

What I Did For Myself Today:

What I Did For Myself Today:

OUR MOST RECENT EPIC MOMENT

Date:

HIS

Today's Goal/s:

What I Want God To Know About Us:

What I Promise Her Today:

What I Want Her To Know Today:

I Am Grateful For Her Because:

It's Important To Me That You:

It's Important To Me That We:

What I Need Today:

What I Did For Myself Today:

HER

Today's Goal/s:

What I Want God To Know About Us:

What I Promise Him Today:

What I Want Him To Know Today:

I Am Grateful For Him Because:

It's Important To Me That You:

It's Important To Me That We:

What I Need Today:

What I Did For Myself Today:

HIS	**HER**
Today's Goal/s:	Today's Goal/s:
What I Want God To Know About Us:	What I Want God To Know About Us:
What I Promise Her Today:	What I Promise Him Today:
What I Want Her To Know Today:	What I Want Him To Know Today:
I Am Grateful For Her Because:	I Am Grateful For Him Because:
It's Important To Me That You:	It's Important To Me That You:
It's Important To Me That We:	It's Important To Me That We:
What I Need Today:	What I Need Today:
What I Did For Myself Today:	What I Did For Myself Today:

HIS RESPONSE:
(What Qualities Do I Possess That Make Me Special To You?)

HER RESPONSE:
(What Qualities Do I Possess That Make Me Special To You?)

Date:

HIS

Today's Goal/s:

What I Want God To Know About Us:

What I Promise Her Today:

What I Want Her To Know Today:

I Am Grateful For Her Because:

It's Important To Me That You:

It's Important To Me That We:

What I Need Today:

What I Did For Myself Today:

HER

Today's Goal/s:

What I Want God To Know About Us:

What I Promise Him Today:

What I Want Him To Know Today:

I Am Grateful For Him Because:

It's Important To Me That You:

It's Important To Me That We:

What I Need Today:

What I Did For Myself Today:

HIS

Today's Goal/s:

What I Want God To Know About Us:

What I Promise Her Today:

What I Want Her To Know Today:

I Am Grateful For Her Because:

It's Important To Me That You:

It's Important To Me That We:

What I Need Today:

What I Did For Myself Today:

HER

Today's Goal/s:

What I Want God To Know About Us:

What I Promise Him Today:

What I Want Him To Know Today:

I Am Grateful For Him Because:

It's Important To Me That You:

It's Important To Me That We:

What I Need Today:

What I Did For Myself Today:

OURS.

My Favorite Love Story.

Date:

HIS

Today's Goal/s:

What I Want God To Know About Us:

What I Promise Her Today:

What I Want Her To Know Today:

I Am Grateful For Her Because:

It's Important To Me That You:

It's Important To Me That We:

What I Need Today:

What I Did For Myself Today:

HER

Today's Goal/s:

What I Want God To Know About Us:

What I Promise Him Today:

What I Want Him To Know Today:

I Am Grateful For Him Because:

It's Important To Me That You:

It's Important To Me That We:

What I Need Today:

What I Did For Myself Today:

Date:

HIS

HER

Today's Goal/s:

Today's Goal/s:

What I Want God To Know About Us:

What I Want God To Know About Us:

What I Promise Her Today:

What I Promise Him Today:

What I Want Her To Know Today:

What I Want Him To Know Today:

I Am Grateful For Her Because:

I Am Grateful For Him Because:

It's Important To Me That You:

It's Important To Me That You:

It's Important To Me That We:

It's Important To Me That We:

What I Need Today:

What I Need Today:

What I Did For Myself Today:

What I Did For Myself Today:

Date:

HIS

Today's Goal/s:

What I Want God To Know About Us:

What I Promise Her Today:

What I Want Her To Know Today:

I Am Grateful For Her Because:

It's Important To Me That You:

It's Important To Me That We:

What I Need Today:

What I Did For Myself Today:

HER

Today's Goal/s:

What I Want God To Know About Us:

What I Promise Him Today:

What I Want Him To Know Today:

I Am Grateful For Him Because:

It's Important To Me That You:

It's Important To Me That We:

What I Need Today:

What I Did For Myself Today:

TODAY'S MAIN QUESTION FOR HIM:

HIS ANSWER:

Date:

HIS

Today's Goal/s:

What I Want God To Know About Us:

What I Promise Her Today:

What I Want Her To Know Today:

I Am Grateful For Her Because:

It's Important To Me That You:

It's Important To Me That We:

What I Need Today:

What I Did For Myself Today:

HER

Today's Goal/s:

What I Want God To Know About Us:

What I Promise Him Today:

What I Want Him To Know Today:

I Am Grateful For Him Because:

It's Important To Me That You:

It's Important To Me That We:

What I Need Today:

What I Did For Myself Today:

HIS

HER

Today's Goal/s:

Today's Goal/s:

What I Want God To Know About Us:

What I Want God To Know About Us:

What I Promise Her Today:

What I Promise Him Today:

What I Want Her To Know Today:

What I Want Him To Know Today:

I Am Grateful For Her Because:

I Am Grateful For Him Because:

It's Important To Me That You:

It's Important To Me That You:

It's Important To Me That We:

It's Important To Me That We:

What I Need Today:

What I Need Today:

What I Did For Myself Today:

What I Did For Myself Today:

Date:

HIS

Today's Goal/s:

What I Want God To Know About Us:

What I Promise Her Today:

What I Want Her To Know Today:

I Am Grateful For Her Because:

It's Important To Me That You:

It's Important To Me That We:

What I Need Today:

What I Did For Myself Today:

HER

Today's Goal/s:

What I Want God To Know About Us:

What I Promise Him Today:

What I Want Him To Know Today:

I Am Grateful For Him Because:

It's Important To Me That You:

It's Important To Me That We:

What I Need Today:

What I Did For Myself Today:

Date:

HIS

Today's Goal/s:

What I Want God To Know About Us:

What I Promise Her Today:

What I Want Her To Know Today:

I Am Grateful For Her Because:

It's Important To Me That You:

It's Important To Me That We:

What I Need Today:

What I Did For Myself Today:

HER

Today's Goal/s:

What I Want God To Know About Us:

What I Promise Him Today:

What I Want Him To Know Today:

I Am Grateful For Him Because:

It's Important To Me That You:

It's Important To Me That We:

What I Need Today:

What I Did For Myself Today:

HIS	**HER**
Today's Goal/s:	Today's Goal/s:
What I Want God To Know About Us:	What I Want God To Know About Us:
What I Promise Her Today:	What I Promise Him Today:
What I Want Her To Know Today:	What I Want Him To Know Today:
I Am Grateful For Her Because:	I Am Grateful For Him Because:
It's Important To Me That You:	It's Important To Me That You:
It's Important To Me That We:	It's Important To Me That We:
What I Need Today:	What I Need Today:
What I Did For Myself Today:	What I Did For Myself Today:

I WILL ALWAYS BE HERE TO SUPPORT YOU.

I Will Always Be Here To Love You.

ALWAYS.

Date:

HIS

Today's Goal/s:

What I Want God To Know About Us:

What I Promise Her Today:

What I Want Her To Know Today:

I Am Grateful For Her Because:

It's Important To Me That You:

It's Important To Me That We:

What I Need Today:

What I Did For Myself Today:

HER

Today's Goal/s:

What I Want God To Know About Us:

What I Promise Him Today:

What I Want Him To Know Today:

I Am Grateful For Him Because:

It's Important To Me That You:

It's Important To Me That We:

What I Need Today:

What I Did For Myself Today:

Date:

HIS	**HER**
Today's Goal/s:	Today's Goal/s:
What I Want God To Know About Us:	What I Want God To Know About Us:
What I Promise Her Today:	What I Promise Him Today:
What I Want Her To Know Today:	What I Want Him To Know Today:
I Am Grateful For Her Because:	I Am Grateful For Him Because:
It's Important To Me That You:	It's Important To Me That You:
It's Important To Me That We:	It's Important To Me That We:
What I Need Today:	What I Need Today:
What I Did For Myself Today:	What I Did For Myself Today:

Date:

HIS

Today's Goal/s:

What I Want God To Know About Us:

What I Promise Her Today:

What I Want Her To Know Today:

I Am Grateful For Her Because:

It's Important To Me That You:

It's Important To Me That We:

What I Need Today:

What I Did For Myself Today:

HER

Today's Goal/s:

What I Want God To Know About Us:

What I Promise Him Today:

What I Want Him To Know Today:

I Am Grateful For Him Because:

It's Important To Me That You:

It's Important To Me That We:

What I Need Today:

What I Did For Myself Today:

Date:

HIS

Today's Goal/s:

What I Want God To Know About Us:

What I Promise Her Today:

What I Want Her To Know Today:

I Am Grateful For Her Because:

It's Important To Me That You:

It's Important To Me That We:

What I Need Today:

What I Did For Myself Today:

HER

Today's Goal/s:

What I Want God To Know About Us:

What I Promise Him Today:

What I Want Him To Know Today:

I Am Grateful For Him Because:

It's Important To Me That You:

It's Important To Me That We:

What I Need Today:

What I Did For Myself Today:

SEVEN THINGS WE HAVE IN COMMON

1.

2.

3.

4.

5.

6.

7.

Date:

HIS

Today's Goal/s:

What I Want God To Know About Us:

What I Promise Her Today:

What I Want Her To Know Today:

I Am Grateful For Her Because:

It's Important To Me That You:

It's Important To Me That We:

What I Need Today:

What I Did For Myself Today:

HER

Today's Goal/s:

What I Want God To Know About Us:

What I Promise Him Today:

What I Want Him To Know Today:

I Am Grateful For Him Because:

It's Important To Me That You:

It's Important To Me That We:

What I Need Today:

What I Did For Myself Today:

Date:

HIS

Today's Goal/s:

What I Want God To Know About Us:

What I Promise Her Today:

What I Want Her To Know Today:

I Am Grateful For Her Because:

It's Important To Me That You:

It's Important To Me That We:

What I Need Today:

What I Did For Myself Today:

HER

Today's Goal/s:

What I Want God To Know About Us:

What I Promise Him Today:

What I Want Him To Know Today:

I Am Grateful For Him Because:

It's Important To Me That You:

It's Important To Me That We:

What I Need Today:

What I Did For Myself Today:

LOVE IN PROGRESS
Date:

HIS

Today's Goal/s:

What I Want God To Know About Us:

What I Promise Her Today:

What I Want Her To Know Today:

I Am Grateful For Her Because:

It's Important To Me That You:

It's Important To Me That We:

What I Need Today:

What I Did For Myself Today:

HER

Today's Goal/s:

What I Want God To Know About Us:

What I Promise Him Today:

What I Want Him To Know Today:

I Am Grateful For Him Because:

It's Important To Me That You:

It's Important To Me That We:

What I Need Today:

What I Did For Myself Today:

Date:

HIS	**HER**
Today's Goal/s:	Today's Goal/s:
What I Want God To Know About Us:	What I Want God To Know About Us:
What I Promise Her Today:	What I Promise Him Today:
What I Want Her To Know Today:	What I Want Him To Know Today:
I Am Grateful For Her Because:	I Am Grateful For Him Because:
It's Important To Me That You:	It's Important To Me That You:
It's Important To Me That We:	It's Important To Me That We:
What I Need Today:	What I Need Today:
What I Did For Myself Today:	What I Did For Myself Today:

We

Really Are Just

Passionate

Friends

Who Fell In Love.

HIS

Today's Goal/s:

What I Want God To Know About Us:

What I Promise Her Today:

What I Want Her To Know Today:

I Am Grateful For Her Because:

It's Important To Me That You:

It's Important To Me That We:

What I Need Today:

What I Did For Myself Today:

HER

Today's Goal/s:

What I Want God To Know About Us:

What I Promise Him Today:

What I Want Him To Know Today:

I Am Grateful For Him Because:

It's Important To Me That You:

It's Important To Me That We:

What I Need Today:

What I Did For Myself Today:

Date:

HIS

Today's Goal/s:

What I Want God To Know About Us:

What I Promise Her Today:

What I Want Her To Know Today:

I Am Grateful For Her Because:

It's Important To Me That You:

It's Important To Me That We:

What I Need Today:

What I Did For Myself Today:

HER

Today's Goal/s:

What I Want God To Know About Us:

What I Promise Him Today:

What I Want Him To Know Today:

I Am Grateful For Him Because:

It's Important To Me That You:

It's Important To Me That We:

What I Need Today:

What I Did For Myself Today:

Date:

HIS

Today's Goal/s:

What I Want God To Know About Us:

What I Promise Her Today:

What I Want Her To Know Today:

I Am Grateful For Her Because:

It's Important To Me That You:

It's Important To Me That We:

What I Need Today:

What I Did For Myself Today:

HER

Today's Goal/s:

What I Want God To Know About Us:

What I Promise Him Today:

What I Want Him To Know Today:

I Am Grateful For Him Because:

It's Important To Me That You:

It's Important To Me That We:

What I Need Today:

What I Did For Myself Today:

Date:

HIS

Today's Goal/s:

What I Want God To Know About Us:

What I Promise Her Today:

What I Want Her To Know Today:

I Am Grateful For Her Because:

It's Important To Me That You:

It's Important To Me That We:

What I Need Today:

What I Did For Myself Today:

HER

Today's Goal/s:

What I Want God To Know About Us:

What I Promise Him Today:

What I Want Him To Know Today:

I Am Grateful For Him Because:

It's Important To Me That You:

It's Important To Me That We:

What I Need Today:

What I Did For Myself Today:

HIS RESPONSE:
(What Is Your Most Common Thought About Me When You Think About Me During The Day?)

HER RESPONSE:
(What Is Your Most Common Thought About Me When You Think About Me During The Day?)

Date:

HIS

Today's Goal/s:

What I Want God To Know About Us:

What I Promise Her Today:

What I Want Her To Know Today:

I Am Grateful For Her Because:

It's Important To Me That You:

It's Important To Me That We:

What I Need Today:

What I Did For Myself Today:

HER

Today's Goal/s:

What I Want God To Know About Us:

What I Promise Him Today:

What I Want Him To Know Today:

I Am Grateful For Him Because:

It's Important To Me That You:

It's Important To Me That We:

What I Need Today:

What I Did For Myself Today:

LOVE IN PROGRESS

Date:

HIS	**HER**
Today's Goal/s:	Today's Goal/s:
What I Want God To Know About Us:	What I Want God To Know About Us:
What I Promise Her Today:	What I Promise Him Today:
What I Want Her To Know Today:	What I Want Him To Know Today:
I Am Grateful For Her Because:	I Am Grateful For Him Because:
It's Important To Me That You:	It's Important To Me That You:
It's Important To Me That We:	It's Important To Me That We:
What I Need Today:	What I Need Today:
What I Did For Myself Today:	What I Did For Myself Today:

Date:

HIS

Today's Goal/s:

What I Want God To Know About Us:

What I Promise Her Today:

What I Want Her To Know Today:

I Am Grateful For Her Because:

It's Important To Me That You:

It's Important To Me That We:

What I Need Today:

What I Did For Myself Today:

HER

Today's Goal/s:

What I Want God To Know About Us:

What I Promise Him Today:

What I Want Him To Know Today:

I Am Grateful For Him Because:

It's Important To Me That You:

It's Important To Me That We:

What I Need Today:

What I Did For Myself Today:

HIS	**HER**
Today's Goal/s:	Today's Goal/s:
What I Want God To Know About Us:	What I Want God To Know About Us:
What I Promise Her Today:	What I Promise Him Today:
What I Want Her To Know Today:	What I Want Him To Know Today:
I Am Grateful For Her Because:	I Am Grateful For Him Because:
It's Important To Me That You:	It's Important To Me That You:
It's Important To Me That We:	It's Important To Me That We:
What I Need Today:	What I Need Today:
What I Did For Myself Today:	What I Did For Myself Today:

You

Make Me Better.

We Will Reach Our Dreams Together.

HIS

Today's Goal/s:

What I Want God To Know About Us:

What I Promise Her Today:

What I Want Her To Know Today:

I Am Grateful For Her Because:

It's Important To Me That You:

It's Important To Me That We:

What I Need Today:

What I Did For Myself Today:

HER

Today's Goal/s:

What I Want God To Know About Us:

What I Promise Him Today:

What I Want Him To Know Today:

I Am Grateful For Him Because:

It's Important To Me That You:

It's Important To Me That We:

What I Need Today:

What I Did For Myself Today:

Date:

HIS

Today's Goal/s:

What I Want God To Know About Us:

What I Promise Her Today:

What I Want Her To Know Today:

I Am Grateful For Her Because:

It's Important To Me That You:

It's Important To Me That We:

What I Need Today:

What I Did For Myself Today:

HER

Today's Goal/s:

What I Want God To Know About Us:

What I Promise Him Today:

What I Want Him To Know Today:

I Am Grateful For Him Because:

It's Important To Me That You:

It's Important To Me That We:

What I Need Today:

What I Did For Myself Today:

LOVE IN PROGRESS
Date:

HIS	**HER**
Today's Goal/s:	Today's Goal/s:
What I Want God To Know About Us:	What I Want God To Know About Us:
What I Promise Her Today:	What I Promise Him Today:
What I Want Her To Know Today:	What I Want Him To Know Today:
I Am Grateful For Her Because:	I Am Grateful For Him Because:
It's Important To Me That You:	It's Important To Me That You:
It's Important To Me That We:	It's Important To Me That We:
What I Need Today:	What I Need Today:
What I Did For Myself Today:	What I Did For Myself Today:

Date:

HIS

Today's Goal/s:

What I Want God To Know About Us:

What I Promise Her Today:

What I Want Her To Know Today:

I Am Grateful For Her Because:

It's Important To Me That You:

It's Important To Me That We:

What I Need Today:

What I Did For Myself Today:

HER

Today's Goal/s:

What I Want God To Know About Us:

What I Promise Him Today:

What I Want Him To Know Today:

I Am Grateful For Him Because:

It's Important To Me That You:

It's Important To Me That We:

What I Need Today:

What I Did For Myself Today:

HIS RESPONSE:
(What Do You Value Most About Our Relationship?)

HER RESPONSE:
(What Do You Value Most About Our Relationship?)

LOVE IN PROGRESS

Date:

HIS	**HER**
Today's Goal/s:	Today's Goal/s:
What I Want God To Know About Us:	What I Want God To Know About Us:
What I Promise Her Today:	What I Promise Him Today:
What I Want Her To Know Today:	What I Want Him To Know Today:
I Am Grateful For Her Because:	I Am Grateful For Him Because:
It's Important To Me That You:	It's Important To Me That You:
It's Important To Me That We:	It's Important To Me That We:
What I Need Today:	What I Need Today:
What I Did For Myself Today:	What I Did For Myself Today:

I

will Continue

TO PRAY

That We Will Grow
With Each Other

Date:

HIS

Today's Goal/s:

What I Want God To Know About Us:

What I Promise Her Today:

What I Want Her To Know Today:

I Am Grateful For Her Because:

It's Important To Me That You:

It's Important To Me That We:

What I Need Today:

What I Did For Myself Today:

HER

Today's Goal/s:

What I Want God To Know About Us:

What I Promise Him Today:

What I Want Him To Know Today:

I Am Grateful For Him Because:

It's Important To Me That You:

It's Important To Me That We:

What I Need Today:

What I Did For Myself Today:

HIS

HER

Today's Goal/s:

Today's Goal/s:

What I Want God To Know About Us:

What I Want God To Know About Us:

What I Promise Her Today:

What I Promise Him Today:

What I Want Her To Know Today:

What I Want Him To Know Today:

I Am Grateful For Her Because:

I Am Grateful For Him Because:

It's Important To Me That You:

It's Important To Me That You:

It's Important To Me That We:

It's Important To Me That We:

What I Need Today:

What I Need Today:

What I Did For Myself Today:

What I Did For Myself Today:

Date:

HIS

Today's Goal/s:

What I Want God To Know About Us:

What I Promise Her Today:

What I Want Her To Know Today:

I Am Grateful For Her Because:

It's Important To Me That You:

It's Important To Me That We:

What I Need Today:

What I Did For Myself Today:

HER

Today's Goal/s:

What I Want God To Know About Us:

What I Promise Him Today:

What I Want Him To Know Today:

I Am Grateful For Him Because:

It's Important To Me That You:

It's Important To Me That We:

What I Need Today:

What I Did For Myself Today:

Date:

HIS

Today's Goal/s:

What I Want God To Know About Us:

What I Promise Her Today:

What I Want Her To Know Today:

I Am Grateful For Her Because:

It's Important To Me That You:

It's Important To Me That We:

What I Need Today:

What I Did For Myself Today:

HER

Today's Goal/s:

What I Want God To Know About Us:

What I Promise Him Today:

What I Want Him To Know Today:

I Am Grateful For Him Because:

It's Important To Me That You:

It's Important To Me That We:

What I Need Today:

What I Did For Myself Today:

Date:

HIS

Today's Goal/s:

What I Want God To Know About Us:

What I Promise Her Today:

What I Want Her To Know Today:

I Am Grateful For Her Because:

It's Important To Me That You:

It's Important To Me That We:

What I Need Today:

What I Did For Myself Today:

HER

Today's Goal/s:

What I Want God To Know About Us:

What I Promise Him Today:

What I Want Him To Know Today:

I Am Grateful For Him Because:

It's Important To Me That You:

It's Important To Me That We:

What I Need Today:

What I Did For Myself Today:

HIS RESPONSE:
(What Is Your Idea Of A Perfect Date Night?)

HER RESPONSE:
(What Is Your Idea Of A Perfect Date Night?)

Date:

HIS

Today's Goal/s:

What I Want God To Know About Us:

What I Promise Her Today:

What I Want Her To Know Today:

I Am Grateful For Her Because:

It's Important To Me That You:

It's Important To Me That We:

What I Need Today:

What I Did For Myself Today:

HER

Today's Goal/s:

What I Want God To Know About Us:

What I Promise Him Today:

What I Want Him To Know Today:

I Am Grateful For Him Because:

It's Important To Me That You:

It's Important To Me That We:

What I Need Today:

What I Did For Myself Today:

LOVE IN PROGRESS
Date:

HIS	**HER**
Today's Goal/s:	Today's Goal/s:
What I Want God To Know About Us:	What I Want God To Know About Us:
What I Promise Her Today:	What I Promise Him Today:
What I Want Her To Know Today:	What I Want Him To Know Today:
I Am Grateful For Her Because:	I Am Grateful For Him Because:
It's Important To Me That You:	It's Important To Me That You:
It's Important To Me That We:	It's Important To Me That We:
What I Need Today:	What I Need Today:
What I Did For Myself Today:	What I Did For Myself Today:

HIS

Today's Goal/s:

What I Want God To Know About Us:

What I Promise Her Today:

What I Want Her To Know Today:

I Am Grateful For Her Because:

It's Important To Me That You:

It's Important To Me That We:

What I Need Today:

What I Did For Myself Today:

HER

Today's Goal/s:

What I Want God To Know About Us:

What I Promise Him Today:

What I Want Him To Know Today:

I Am Grateful For Him Because:

It's Important To Me That You:

It's Important To Me That We:

What I Need Today:

What I Did For Myself Today:

AFTER GOD...

I Prefer You & Me.

Date:

HIS

Today's Goal/s:

What I Want God To Know About Us:

What I Promise Her Today:

What I Want Her To Know Today:

I Am Grateful For Her Because:

It's Important To Me That You:

It's Important To Me That We:

What I Need Today:

What I Did For Myself Today:

HER

Today's Goal/s:

What I Want God To Know About Us:

What I Promise Him Today:

What I Want Him To Know Today:

I Am Grateful For Him Because:

It's Important To Me That You:

It's Important To Me That We:

What I Need Today:

What I Did For Myself Today:

HIS

Today's Goal/s:

What I Want God To Know About Us:

What I Promise Her Today:

What I Want Her To Know Today:

I Am Grateful For Her Because:

It's Important To Me That You:

It's Important To Me That We:

What I Need Today:

What I Did For Myself Today:

HER

Today's Goal/s:

What I Want God To Know About Us:

What I Promise Him Today:

What I Want Him To Know Today:

I Am Grateful For Him Because:

It's Important To Me That You:

It's Important To Me That We:

What I Need Today:

What I Did For Myself Today:

Date:

HIS

Today's Goal/s:

What I Want God To Know About Us:

What I Promise Her Today:

What I Want Her To Know Today:

I Am Grateful For Her Because:

It's Important To Me That You:

It's Important To Me That We:

What I Need Today:

What I Did For Myself Today:

HER

Today's Goal/s:

What I Want God To Know About Us:

What I Promise Him Today:

What I Want Him To Know Today:

I Am Grateful For Him Because:

It's Important To Me That You:

It's Important To Me That We:

What I Need Today:

What I Did For Myself Today:

Date:

HIS

Today's Goal/s:

What I Want God To Know About Us:

What I Promise Her Today:

What I Want Her To Know Today:

I Am Grateful For Her Because:

It's Important To Me That You:

It's Important To Me That We:

What I Need Today:

What I Did For Myself Today:

HER

Today's Goal/s:

What I Want God To Know About Us:

What I Promise Him Today:

What I Want Him To Know Today:

I Am Grateful For Him Because:

It's Important To Me That You:

It's Important To Me That We:

What I Need Today:

What I Did For Myself Today:

Date:

HIS

Today's Goal/s:

What I Want God To Know About Us:

What I Promise Her Today:

What I Want Her To Know Today:

I Am Grateful For Her Because:

It's Important To Me That You:

It's Important To Me That We:

What I Need Today:

What I Did For Myself Today:

HER

Today's Goal/s:

What I Want God To Know About Us:

What I Promise Him Today:

What I Want Him To Know Today:

I Am Grateful For Him Because:

It's Important To Me That You:

It's Important To Me That We:

What I Need Today:

What I Did For Myself Today:

HIS

Today's Goal/s:

What I Want God To Know About Us:

What I Promise Her Today:

What I Want Her To Know Today:

I Am Grateful For Her Because:

It's Important To Me That You:

It's Important To Me That We:

What I Need Today:

What I Did For Myself Today:

HER

Today's Goal/s:

What I Want God To Know About Us:

What I Promise Him Today:

What I Want Him To Know Today:

I Am Grateful For Him Because:

It's Important To Me That You:

It's Important To Me That We:

What I Need Today:

What I Did For Myself Today:

HIS RESPONSE:
(One Word That Describes Our Relationship)

HER RESPONSE:
(One Word That Describes Our Relationship)

Date:

HIS   ## HER

Today's Goal/s: Today's Goal/s:

What I Want God To Know About Us: What I Want God To Know About Us:

What I Promise Her Today: What I Promise Him Today:

What I Want Her To Know Today: What I Want Him To Know Today:

I Am Grateful For Her Because: I Am Grateful For Him Because:

It's Important To Me That You: It's Important To Me That You:

It's Important To Me That We: It's Important To Me That We:

What I Need Today: What I Need Today:

What I Did For Myself Today: What I Did For Myself Today:

LOVE IN PROGRESS
Date:

HIS	**HER**
Today's Goal/s:	Today's Goal/s:
What I Want God To Know About Us:	What I Want God To Know About Us:
What I Promise Her Today:	What I Promise Him Today:
What I Want Her To Know Today:	What I Want Him To Know Today:
I Am Grateful For Her Because:	I Am Grateful For Him Because:
It's Important To Me That You:	It's Important To Me That You:
It's Important To Me That We:	It's Important To Me That We:
What I Need Today:	What I Need Today:
What I Did For Myself Today:	What I Did For Myself Today:

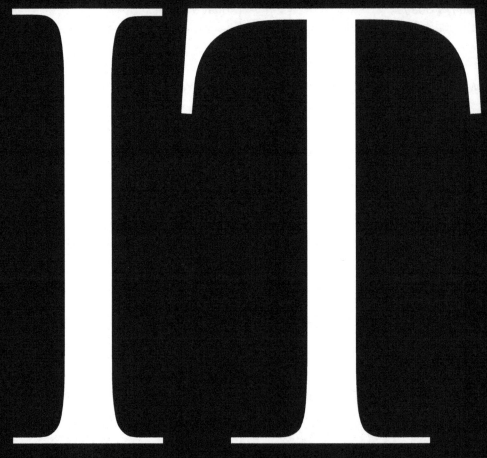

IT

Doesn't Matter

What Happens In Life, As Long
As Our Love Is A Priority.

Date:

HIS

Today's Goal/s:

What I Want God To Know About Us:

What I Promise Her Today:

What I Want Her To Know Today:

I Am Grateful For Her Because:

It's Important To Me That You:

It's Important To Me That We:

What I Need Today:

What I Did For Myself Today:

HER

Today's Goal/s:

What I Want God To Know About Us:

What I Promise Him Today:

What I Want Him To Know Today:

I Am Grateful For Him Because:

It's Important To Me That You:

It's Important To Me That We:

What I Need Today:

What I Did For Myself Today:

LOVE IN PROGRESS

Date:

HIS	**HER**
Today's Goal/s:	Today's Goal/s:
What I Want God To Know About Us:	What I Want God To Know About Us:
What I Promise Her Today:	What I Promise Him Today:
What I Want Her To Know Today:	What I Want Him To Know Today:
I Am Grateful For Her Because:	I Am Grateful For Him Because:
It's Important To Me That You:	It's Important To Me That You:
It's Important To Me That We:	It's Important To Me That We:
What I Need Today:	What I Need Today:
What I Did For Myself Today:	What I Did For Myself Today:

Date:

HIS

Today's Goal/s:

What I Want God To Know About Us:

What I Promise Her Today:

What I Want Her To Know Today:

I Am Grateful For Her Because:

It's Important To Me That You:

It's Important To Me That We:

What I Need Today:

What I Did For Myself Today:

HER

Today's Goal/s:

What I Want God To Know About Us:

What I Promise Him Today:

What I Want Him To Know Today:

I Am Grateful For Him Because:

It's Important To Me That You:

It's Important To Me That We:

What I Need Today:

What I Did For Myself Today:

Date:

HIS

Today's Goal/s:

What I Want God To Know About Us:

What I Promise Her Today:

What I Want Her To Know Today:

I Am Grateful For Her Because:

It's Important To Me That You:

It's Important To Me That We:

What I Need Today:

What I Did For Myself Today:

HER

Today's Goal/s:

What I Want God To Know About Us:

What I Promise Him Today:

What I Want Him To Know Today:

I Am Grateful For Him Because:

It's Important To Me That You:

It's Important To Me That We:

What I Need Today:

What I Did For Myself Today:

Date:

HIS

Today's Goal/s:

What I Want God To Know About Us:

What I Promise Her Today:

What I Want Her To Know Today:

I Am Grateful For Her Because:

It's Important To Me That You:

It's Important To Me That We:

What I Need Today:

What I Did For Myself Today:

HER

Today's Goal/s:

What I Want God To Know About Us:

What I Promise Him Today:

What I Want Him To Know Today:

I Am Grateful For Him Because:

It's Important To Me That You:

It's Important To Me That We:

What I Need Today:

What I Did For Myself Today:

LOVE IN PROGRESS
Date:

HIS	**HER**
Today's Goal/s:	Today's Goal/s:
What I Want God To Know About Us:	What I Want God To Know About Us:
What I Promise Her Today:	What I Promise Him Today:
What I Want Her To Know Today:	What I Want Him To Know Today:
I Am Grateful For Her Because:	I Am Grateful For Him Because:
It's Important To Me That You:	It's Important To Me That You:
It's Important To Me That We:	It's Important To Me That We:
What I Need Today:	What I Need Today:
What I Did For Myself Today:	What I Did For Myself Today:

A PRAYER FOR HIM:

A PRAYER FOR HER:

LOVE IN PROGRESS

Date:

HIS	**HER**
Today's Goal/s:	Today's Goal/s:
What I Want God To Know About Us:	What I Want God To Know About Us:
What I Promise Her Today:	What I Promise Him Today:
What I Want Her To Know Today:	What I Want Him To Know Today:
I Am Grateful For Her Because:	I Am Grateful For Him Because:
It's Important To Me That You:	It's Important To Me That You:
It's Important To Me That We:	It's Important To Me That We:
What I Need Today:	What I Need Today:
What I Did For Myself Today:	What I Did For Myself Today:

E

VERYDAY

I Am Learning To Love You As
Much As God Loves You.

LOVE IN PROGRESS
Date:

HIS	**HER**
Today's Goal/s:	Today's Goal/s:
What I Want God To Know About Us:	What I Want God To Know About Us:
What I Promise Her Today:	What I Promise Him Today:
What I Want Her To Know Today:	What I Want Him To Know Today:
I Am Grateful For Her Because:	I Am Grateful For Him Because:
It's Important To Me That You:	It's Important To Me That You:
It's Important To Me That We:	It's Important To Me That We:
What I Need Today:	What I Need Today:
What I Did For Myself Today:	What I Did For Myself Today:

Date:

HIS	**HER**
Today's Goal/s:	Today's Goal/s:
What I Want God To Know About Us:	What I Want God To Know About Us:
What I Promise Her Today:	What I Promise Him Today:
What I Want Her To Know Today:	What I Want Him To Know Today:
I Am Grateful For Her Because:	I Am Grateful For Him Because:
It's Important To Me That You:	It's Important To Me That You:
It's Important To Me That We:	It's Important To Me That We:
What I Need Today:	What I Need Today:
What I Did For Myself Today:	What I Did For Myself Today:

LOVE IN PROGRESS
Date:

HIS	**HER**
Today's Goal/s:	Today's Goal/s:
What I Want God To Know About Us:	What I Want God To Know About Us:
What I Promise Her Today:	What I Promise Him Today:
What I Want Her To Know Today:	What I Want Him To Know Today:
I Am Grateful For Her Because:	I Am Grateful For Him Because:
It's Important To Me That You:	It's Important To Me That You:
It's Important To Me That We:	It's Important To Me That We:
What I Need Today:	What I Need Today:
What I Did For Myself Today:	What I Did For Myself Today:

HIS RESPONSE:
(Tell Me One Thing You Would Like To Confess To Me)

HER RESPONSE:
(Tell Me One Thing You Would Like To Confess To Me)

Date:

HIS

Today's Goal/s:

What I Want God To Know About Us:

What I Promise Her Today:

What I Want Her To Know Today:

I Am Grateful For Her Because:

It's Important To Me That You:

It's Important To Me That We:

What I Need Today:

What I Did For Myself Today:

HER

Today's Goal/s:

What I Want God To Know About Us:

What I Promise Him Today:

What I Want Him To Know Today:

I Am Grateful For Him Because:

It's Important To Me That You:

It's Important To Me That We:

What I Need Today:

What I Did For Myself Today:

Date:

HIS

Today's Goal/s:

What I Want God To Know About Us:

What I Promise Her Today:

What I Want Her To Know Today:

I Am Grateful For Her Because:

It's Important To Me That You:

It's Important To Me That We:

What I Need Today:

What I Did For Myself Today:

HER

Today's Goal/s:

What I Want God To Know About Us:

What I Promise Him Today:

What I Want Him To Know Today:

I Am Grateful For Him Because:

It's Important To Me That You:

It's Important To Me That We:

What I Need Today:

What I Did For Myself Today:

HIS	**HER**
Today's Goal/s:	Today's Goal/s:
What I Want God To Know About Us:	What I Want God To Know About Us:
What I Promise Her Today:	What I Promise Him Today:
What I Want Her To Know Today:	What I Want Him To Know Today:
I Am Grateful For Her Because:	I Am Grateful For Him Because:
It's Important To Me That You:	It's Important To Me That You:
It's Important To Me That We:	It's Important To Me That We:
What I Need Today:	What I Need Today:
What I Did For Myself Today:	What I Did For Myself Today:

I HAVE ENOUGH ROOM IN MY HEART

To Love You.
All Of You.

HIS

Today's Goal/s:

What I Want God To Know About Us:

What I Promise Her Today:

What I Want Her To Know Today:

I Am Grateful For Her Because:

It's Important To Me That You:

It's Important To Me That We:

What I Need Today:

What I Did For Myself Today:

HER

Today's Goal/s:

What I Want God To Know About Us:

What I Promise Him Today:

What I Want Him To Know Today:

I Am Grateful For Him Because:

It's Important To Me That You:

It's Important To Me That We:

What I Need Today:

What I Did For Myself Today:

Date:

HIS

Today's Goal/s:

What I Want God To Know About Us:

What I Promise Her Today:

What I Want Her To Know Today:

I Am Grateful For Her Because:

It's Important To Me That You:

It's Important To Me That We:

What I Need Today:

What I Did For Myself Today:

HER

Today's Goal/s:

What I Want God To Know About Us:

What I Promise Him Today:

What I Want Him To Know Today:

I Am Grateful For Him Because:

It's Important To Me That You:

It's Important To Me That We:

What I Need Today:

What I Did For Myself Today:

HIS

Today's Goal/s:

What I Want God To Know About Us:

What I Promise Her Today:

What I Want Her To Know Today:

I Am Grateful For Her Because:

It's Important To Me That You:

It's Important To Me That We:

What I Need Today:

What I Did For Myself Today:

HER

Today's Goal/s:

What I Want God To Know About Us:

What I Promise Him Today:

What I Want Him To Know Today:

I Am Grateful For Him Because:

It's Important To Me That You:

It's Important To Me That We:

What I Need Today:

What I Did For Myself Today:

HIS RESPONSE:
(What Does This Relationship Mean To You?)

HER RESPONSE:
(What Does This Relationship Mean To You?)

HIS

HER

HIS

Today's Goal/s:

What I Want God To Know About Us:

What I Promise Her Today:

What I Want Her To Know Today:

I Am Grateful For Her Because:

It's Important To Me That You:

It's Important To Me That We:

What I Need Today:

What I Did For Myself Today:

HER

Today's Goal/s:

What I Want God To Know About Us:

What I Promise Him Today:

What I Want Him To Know Today:

I Am Grateful For Him Because:

It's Important To Me That You:

It's Important To Me That We:

What I Need Today:

What I Did For Myself Today:

Date:

HIS

Today's Goal/s:

What I Want God To Know About Us:

What I Promise Her Today:

What I Want Her To Know Today:

I Am Grateful For Her Because:

It's Important To Me That You:

It's Important To Me That We:

What I Need Today:

What I Did For Myself Today:

HER

Today's Goal/s:

What I Want God To Know About Us:

What I Promise Him Today:

What I Want Him To Know Today:

I Am Grateful For Him Because:

It's Important To Me That You:

It's Important To Me That We:

What I Need Today:

What I Did For Myself Today:

LOVE IN PROGRESS
Date:

HIS	**HER**
Today's Goal/s:	Today's Goal/s:
What I Want God To Know About Us:	What I Want God To Know About Us:
What I Promise Her Today:	What I Promise Him Today:
What I Want Her To Know Today:	What I Want Him To Know Today:
I Am Grateful For Her Because:	I Am Grateful For Him Because:
It's Important To Me That You:	It's Important To Me That You:
It's Important To Me That We:	It's Important To Me That We:
What I Need Today:	What I Need Today:
What I Did For Myself Today:	What I Did For Myself Today:

IN
YOUR BEST TIMES
IN Your Worst Times

I Won't Let You Go

I Am Here For You

LOVE IN PROGRESS
Date:

HIS	**HER**
Today's Goal/s:	Today's Goal/s:
What I Want God To Know About Us:	What I Want God To Know About Us:
What I Promise Her Today:	What I Promise Him Today:
What I Want Her To Know Today:	What I Want Him To Know Today:
I Am Grateful For Her Because:	I Am Grateful For Him Because:
It's Important To Me That You:	It's Important To Me That You:
It's Important To Me That We:	It's Important To Me That We:
What I Need Today:	What I Need Today:
What I Did For Myself Today:	What I Did For Myself Today:

Date:

HIS

Today's Goal/s:

What I Want God To Know About Us:

What I Promise Her Today:

What I Want Her To Know Today:

I Am Grateful For Her Because:

It's Important To Me That You:

It's Important To Me That We:

What I Need Today:

What I Did For Myself Today:

HER

Today's Goal/s:

What I Want God To Know About Us:

What I Promise Him Today:

What I Want Him To Know Today:

I Am Grateful For Him Because:

It's Important To Me That You:

It's Important To Me That We:

What I Need Today:

What I Did For Myself Today:

Date:

HIS

HER

HIS

Today's Goal/s:

What I Want God To Know About Us:

What I Promise Her Today:

What I Want Her To Know Today:

I Am Grateful For Her Because:

It's Important To Me That You:

It's Important To Me That We:

What I Need Today:

What I Did For Myself Today:

HER

Today's Goal/s:

What I Want God To Know About Us:

What I Promise Him Today:

What I Want Him To Know Today:

I Am Grateful For Him Because:

It's Important To Me That You:

It's Important To Me That We:

What I Need Today:

What I Did For Myself Today:

Date:

HIS

Today's Goal/s:

What I Want God To Know About Us:

What I Promise Her Today:

What I Want Her To Know Today:

I Am Grateful For Her Because:

It's Important To Me That You:

It's Important To Me That We:

What I Need Today:

What I Did For Myself Today:

HER

Today's Goal/s:

What I Want God To Know About Us:

What I Promise Him Today:

What I Want Him To Know Today:

I Am Grateful For Him Because:

It's Important To Me That You:

It's Important To Me That We:

What I Need Today:

What I Did For Myself Today:

LOVE IN PROGRESS
Date:

HIS	**HER**
Today's Goal/s:	Today's Goal/s:
What I Want God To Know About Us:	What I Want God To Know About Us:
What I Promise Her Today:	What I Promise Him Today:
What I Want Her To Know Today:	What I Want Him To Know Today:
I Am Grateful For Her Because:	I Am Grateful For Him Because:
It's Important To Me That You:	It's Important To Me That You:
It's Important To Me That We:	It's Important To Me That We:
What I Need Today:	What I Need Today:
What I Did For Myself Today:	What I Did For Myself Today:

HIS

Today's Goal/s:

What I Want God To Know About Us:

What I Promise Her Today:

What I Want Her To Know Today:

I Am Grateful For Her Because:

It's Important To Me That You:

It's Important To Me That We:

What I Need Today:

What I Did For Myself Today:

HER

Today's Goal/s:

What I Want God To Know About Us:

What I Promise Him Today:

What I Want Him To Know Today:

I Am Grateful For Him Because:

It's Important To Me That You:

It's Important To Me That We:

What I Need Today:

What I Did For Myself Today:

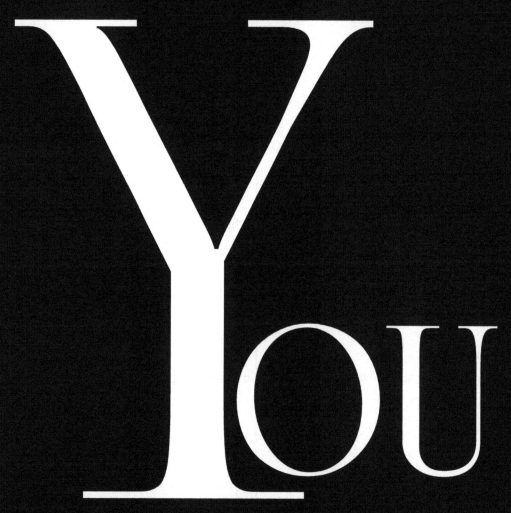

You

Are A Reflection Of Me.
I Like What I See.

Date:

HIS

HER

Today's Goal/s:

Today's Goal/s:

What I Want God To Know About Us:

What I Want God To Know About Us:

What I Promise Her Today:

What I Promise Him Today:

What I Want Her To Know Today:

What I Want Him To Know Today:

I Am Grateful For Her Because:

I Am Grateful For Him Because:

It's Important To Me That You:

It's Important To Me That You:

It's Important To Me That We:

It's Important To Me That We:

What I Need Today:

What I Need Today:

What I Did For Myself Today:

What I Did For Myself Today:

HIS

Today's Goal/s:

What I Want God To Know About Us:

What I Promise Her Today:

What I Want Her To Know Today:

I Am Grateful For Her Because:

It's Important To Me That You:

It's Important To Me That We:

What I Need Today:

What I Did For Myself Today:

HER

Today's Goal/s:

What I Want God To Know About Us:

What I Promise Him Today:

What I Want Him To Know Today:

I Am Grateful For Him Because:

It's Important To Me That You:

It's Important To Me That We:

What I Need Today:

What I Did For Myself Today:

Date:

HIS

Today's Goal/s:

What I Want God To Know About Us:

What I Promise Her Today:

What I Want Her To Know Today:

I Am Grateful For Her Because:

It's Important To Me That You:

It's Important To Me That We:

What I Need Today:

What I Did For Myself Today:

HER

Today's Goal/s:

What I Want God To Know About Us:

What I Promise Him Today:

What I Want Him To Know Today:

I Am Grateful For Him Because:

It's Important To Me That You:

It's Important To Me That We:

What I Need Today:

What I Did For Myself Today:

LOVE IN PROGRESS
Date:

HIS	**HER**
Today's Goal/s:	Today's Goal/s:
What I Want God To Know About Us:	What I Want God To Know About Us:
What I Promise Her Today:	What I Promise Him Today:
What I Want Her To Know Today:	What I Want Him To Know Today:
I Am Grateful For Her Because:	I Am Grateful For Him Because:
It's Important To Me That You:	It's Important To Me That You:
It's Important To Me That We:	It's Important To Me That We:
What I Need Today:	What I Need Today:
What I Did For Myself Today:	What I Did For Myself Today:

HIS RESPONSE:
**(What Does Unconditional Love Mean To You?
What Does It Look Like?)**

HER RESPONSE:
**(What Does Unconditional Love Mean To You?
What Does It Look Like?)**

HIS

Today's Goal/s:

What I Want God To Know About Us:

What I Promise Her Today:

What I Want Her To Know Today:

I Am Grateful For Her Because:

It's Important To Me That You:

It's Important To Me That We:

What I Need Today:

What I Did For Myself Today:

HER

Today's Goal/s:

What I Want God To Know About Us:

What I Promise Him Today:

What I Want Him To Know Today:

I Am Grateful For Him Because:

It's Important To Me That You:

It's Important To Me That We:

What I Need Today:

What I Did For Myself Today:

Date:

HIS

Today's Goal/s:

What I Want God To Know About Us:

What I Promise Her Today:

What I Want Her To Know Today:

I Am Grateful For Her Because:

It's Important To Me That You:

It's Important To Me That We:

What I Need Today:

What I Did For Myself Today:

HER

Today's Goal/s:

What I Want God To Know About Us:

What I Promise Him Today:

What I Want Him To Know Today:

I Am Grateful For Him Because:

It's Important To Me That You:

It's Important To Me That We:

What I Need Today:

What I Did For Myself Today:

HIS RESPONSE:
(What Is One Secret You've Wanted To Tell Me But Haven't?)

HER RESPONSE:
(What Is One Secret You've Wanted To Tell Me But Haven't?)

LOVE IN PROGRESS
Date:

HIS	**HER**
Today's Goal/s:	Today's Goal/s:
What I Want God To Know About Us:	What I Want God To Know About Us:
What I Promise Her Today:	What I Promise Him Today:
What I Want Her To Know Today:	What I Want Him To Know Today:
I Am Grateful For Her Because:	I Am Grateful For Him Because:
It's Important To Me That You:	It's Important To Me That You:
It's Important To Me That We:	It's Important To Me That We:
What I Need Today:	What I Need Today:
What I Did For Myself Today:	What I Did For Myself Today:

HIS

HER

Today's Goal/s:

Today's Goal/s:

What I Want God To Know About Us:

What I Want God To Know About Us:

What I Promise Her Today:

What I Promise Him Today:

What I Want Her To Know Today:

What I Want Him To Know Today:

I Am Grateful For Her Because:

I Am Grateful For Him Because:

It's Important To Me That You:

It's Important To Me That You:

It's Important To Me That We:

It's Important To Me That We:

What I Need Today:

What I Need Today:

What I Did For Myself Today:

What I Did For Myself Today:

Date:

HIS

Today's Goal/s:

What I Want God To Know About Us:

What I Promise Her Today:

What I Want Her To Know Today:

I Am Grateful For Her Because:

It's Important To Me That You:

It's Important To Me That We:

What I Need Today:

What I Did For Myself Today:

HER

Today's Goal/s:

What I Want God To Know About Us:

What I Promise Him Today:

What I Want Him To Know Today:

I Am Grateful For Him Because:

It's Important To Me That You:

It's Important To Me That We:

What I Need Today:

What I Did For Myself Today:

We

Shine Bright Together

Date:

HIS

Today's Goal/s:

What I Want God To Know About Us:

What I Promise Her Today:

What I Want Her To Know Today:

I Am Grateful For Her Because:

It's Important To Me That You:

It's Important To Me That We:

What I Need Today:

What I Did For Myself Today:

HER

Today's Goal/s:

What I Want God To Know About Us:

What I Promise Him Today:

What I Want Him To Know Today:

I Am Grateful For Him Because:

It's Important To Me That You:

It's Important To Me That We:

What I Need Today:

What I Did For Myself Today:

HIS

Today's Goal/s:

What I Want God To Know About Us:

What I Promise Her Today:

What I Want Her To Know Today:

I Am Grateful For Her Because:

It's Important To Me That You:

It's Important To Me That We:

What I Need Today:

What I Did For Myself Today:

HER

Today's Goal/s:

What I Want God To Know About Us:

What I Promise Him Today:

What I Want Him To Know Today:

I Am Grateful For Him Because:

It's Important To Me That You:

It's Important To Me That We:

What I Need Today:

What I Did For Myself Today:

Date:

HIS

Today's Goal/s:

What I Want God To Know About Us:

What I Promise Her Today:

What I Want Her To Know Today:

I Am Grateful For Her Because:

It's Important To Me That You:

It's Important To Me That We:

What I Need Today:

What I Did For Myself Today:

HER

Today's Goal/s:

What I Want God To Know About Us:

What I Promise Him Today:

What I Want Him To Know Today:

I Am Grateful For Him Because:

It's Important To Me That You:

It's Important To Me That We:

What I Need Today:

What I Did For Myself Today:

Date:

HIS	**HER**
Today's Goal/s:	Today's Goal/s:
What I Want God To Know About Us:	What I Want God To Know About Us:
What I Promise Her Today:	What I Promise Him Today:
What I Want Her To Know Today:	What I Want Him To Know Today:
I Am Grateful For Her Because:	I Am Grateful For Him Because:
It's Important To Me That You:	It's Important To Me That You:
It's Important To Me That We:	It's Important To Me That We:
What I Need Today:	What I Need Today:
What I Did For Myself Today:	What I Did For Myself Today:

Date:

HIS

Today's Goal/s:

What I Want God To Know About Us:

What I Promise Her Today:

What I Want Her To Know Today:

I Am Grateful For Her Because:

It's Important To Me That You:

It's Important To Me That We:

What I Need Today:

What I Did For Myself Today:

HER

Today's Goal/s:

What I Want God To Know About Us:

What I Promise Him Today:

What I Want Him To Know Today:

I Am Grateful For Him Because:

It's Important To Me That You:

It's Important To Me That We:

What I Need Today:

What I Did For Myself Today:

Date:

HIS

Today's Goal/s:

What I Want God To Know About Us:

What I Promise Her Today:

What I Want Her To Know Today:

I Am Grateful For Her Because:

It's Important To Me That You:

It's Important To Me That We:

What I Need Today:

What I Did For Myself Today:

HER

Today's Goal/s:

What I Want God To Know About Us:

What I Promise Him Today:

What I Want Him To Know Today:

I Am Grateful For Him Because:

It's Important To Me That You:

It's Important To Me That We:

What I Need Today:

What I Did For Myself Today:

HIS RESPONSE:
(When Was The Last Time I Was In Your Dreams?
What Was The Dream About?)

HER RESPONSE:
(When Was The Last Time I Was In Your Dreams?
What Was The Dream About?)

Date:

HIS

Today's Goal/s:

What I Want God To Know About Us:

What I Promise Her Today:

What I Want Her To Know Today:

I Am Grateful For Her Because:

It's Important To Me That You:

It's Important To Me That We:

What I Need Today:

What I Did For Myself Today:

HER

Today's Goal/s:

What I Want God To Know About Us:

What I Promise Him Today:

What I Want Him To Know Today:

I Am Grateful For Him Because:

It's Important To Me That You:

It's Important To Me That We:

What I Need Today:

What I Did For Myself Today:

Date:

HIS	**HER**
Today's Goal/s:	Today's Goal/s:
What I Want God To Know About Us:	What I Want God To Know About Us:
What I Promise Her Today:	What I Promise Him Today:
What I Want Her To Know Today:	What I Want Him To Know Today:
I Am Grateful For Her Because:	I Am Grateful For Him Because:
It's Important To Me That You:	It's Important To Me That You:
It's Important To Me That We:	It's Important To Me That We:
What I Need Today:	What I Need Today:
What I Did For Myself Today:	What I Did For Myself Today:

HIS

Today's Goal/s:

What I Want God To Know About Us:

What I Promise Her Today:

What I Want Her To Know Today:

I Am Grateful For Her Because:

It's Important To Me That You:

It's Important To Me That We:

What I Need Today:

What I Did For Myself Today:

HER

Today's Goal/s:

What I Want God To Know About Us:

What I Promise Him Today:

What I Want Him To Know Today:

I Am Grateful For Him Because:

It's Important To Me That You:

It's Important To Me That We:

What I Need Today:

What I Did For Myself Today:

Date:

HIS

Today's Goal/s:

What I Want God To Know About Us:

What I Promise Her Today:

What I Want Her To Know Today:

I Am Grateful For Her Because:

It's Important To Me That You:

It's Important To Me That We:

What I Need Today:

What I Did For Myself Today:

HER

Today's Goal/s:

What I Want God To Know About Us:

What I Promise Him Today:

What I Want Him To Know Today:

I Am Grateful For Him Because:

It's Important To Me That You:

It's Important To Me That We:

What I Need Today:

What I Did For Myself Today:

Date:

HIS

Today's Goal/s:

What I Want God To Know About Us:

What I Promise Her Today:

What I Want Her To Know Today:

I Am Grateful For Her Because:

It's Important To Me That You:

It's Important To Me That We:

What I Need Today:

What I Did For Myself Today:

HER

Today's Goal/s:

What I Want God To Know About Us:

What I Promise Him Today:

What I Want Him To Know Today:

I Am Grateful For Him Because:

It's Important To Me That You:

It's Important To Me That We:

What I Need Today:

What I Did For Myself Today:

I
Am
Proud
Of You

HIS

Today's Goal/s:

What I Want God To Know About Us:

What I Promise Her Today:

What I Want Her To Know Today:

I Am Grateful For Her Because:

It's Important To Me That You:

It's Important To Me That We:

What I Need Today:

What I Did For Myself Today:

HER

Today's Goal/s:

What I Want God To Know About Us:

What I Promise Him Today:

What I Want Him To Know Today:

I Am Grateful For Him Because:

It's Important To Me That You:

It's Important To Me That We:

What I Need Today:

What I Did For Myself Today:

Date:

HIS	**HER**
Today's Goal/s:	Today's Goal/s:
What I Want God To Know About Us:	What I Want God To Know About Us:
What I Promise Her Today:	What I Promise Him Today:
What I Want Her To Know Today:	What I Want Him To Know Today:
I Am Grateful For Her Because:	I Am Grateful For Him Because:
It's Important To Me That You:	It's Important To Me That You:
It's Important To Me That We:	It's Important To Me That We:
What I Need Today:	What I Need Today:
What I Did For Myself Today:	What I Did For Myself Today:

HIS RESPONSE:

(If You Can Redo Anything You Did In Our Relationship, What Would It Be?)

HER RESPONSE:

(If You Can Redo Anything You Did In Our Relationship, What Would It Be?)

Date:

HIS

Today's Goal/s:

What I Want God To Know About Us:

What I Promise Her Today:

What I Want Her To Know Today:

I Am Grateful For Her Because:

It's Important To Me That You:

It's Important To Me That We:

What I Need Today:

What I Did For Myself Today:

HER

Today's Goal/s:

What I Want God To Know About Us:

What I Promise Him Today:

What I Want Him To Know Today:

I Am Grateful For Him Because:

It's Important To Me That You:

It's Important To Me That We:

What I Need Today:

What I Did For Myself Today:

Date:

HIS | ## HER

HIS	HER
Today's Goal/s:	Today's Goal/s:
What I Want God To Know About Us:	What I Want God To Know About Us:
What I Promise Her Today:	What I Promise Him Today:
What I Want Her To Know Today:	What I Want Him To Know Today:
I Am Grateful For Her Because:	I Am Grateful For Him Because:
It's Important To Me That You:	It's Important To Me That You:
It's Important To Me That We:	It's Important To Me That We:
What I Need Today:	What I Need Today:
What I Did For Myself Today:	What I Did For Myself Today:

Date:

HIS

Today's Goal/s:

What I Want God To Know About Us:

What I Promise Her Today:

What I Want Her To Know Today:

I Am Grateful For Her Because:

It's Important To Me That You:

It's Important To Me That We:

What I Need Today:

What I Did For Myself Today:

HER

Today's Goal/s:

What I Want God To Know About Us:

What I Promise Him Today:

What I Want Him To Know Today:

I Am Grateful For Him Because:

It's Important To Me That You:

It's Important To Me That We:

What I Need Today:

What I Did For Myself Today:

HIS

Today's Goal/s:

What I Want God To Know About Us:

What I Promise Her Today:

What I Want Her To Know Today:

I Am Grateful For Her Because:

It's Important To Me That You:

It's Important To Me That We:

What I Need Today:

What I Did For Myself Today:

HER

Today's Goal/s:

What I Want God To Know About Us:

What I Promise Him Today:

What I Want Him To Know Today:

I Am Grateful For Him Because:

It's Important To Me That You:

It's Important To Me That We:

What I Need Today:

What I Did For Myself Today:

HIS RESPONSE:
(What Is The Craziest Thing You'd Be Willing To Do For Me?)

HER RESPONSE:
(What Is The Craziest Thing You'd Be Willing To Do For Me?)

LOVE IN PROGRESS
Date:

HIS

Today's Goal/s:

What I Want God To Know About Us:

What I Promise Her Today:

What I Want Her To Know Today:

I Am Grateful For Her Because:

It's Important To Me That You:

It's Important To Me That We:

What I Need Today:

What I Did For Myself Today:

HER

Today's Goal/s:

What I Want God To Know About Us:

What I Promise Him Today:

What I Want Him To Know Today:

I Am Grateful For Him Because:

It's Important To Me That You:

It's Important To Me That We:

What I Need Today:

What I Did For Myself Today:

Date:

HIS

Today's Goal/s:

What I Want God To Know About Us:

What I Promise Her Today:

What I Want Her To Know Today:

I Am Grateful For Her Because:

It's Important To Me That You:

It's Important To Me That We:

What I Need Today:

What I Did For Myself Today:

HER

Today's Goal/s:

What I Want God To Know About Us:

What I Promise Him Today:

What I Want Him To Know Today:

I Am Grateful For Him Because:

It's Important To Me That You:

It's Important To Me That We:

What I Need Today:

What I Did For Myself Today:

FIVE THINGS WE WANT TO DO TOGETHER IN THE NEXT THREE MONTHS

1.

2.

3.

4.

5.

Date:

HIS

Today's Goal/s:

What I Want God To Know About Us:

What I Promise Her Today:

What I Want Her To Know Today:

I Am Grateful For Her Because:

It's Important To Me That You:

It's Important To Me That We:

What I Need Today:

What I Did For Myself Today:

HER

Today's Goal/s:

What I Want God To Know About Us:

What I Promise Him Today:

What I Want Him To Know Today:

I Am Grateful For Him Because:

It's Important To Me That You:

It's Important To Me That We:

What I Need Today:

What I Did For Myself Today:

Date:

HIS

HER

Today's Goal/s:

What I Want God To Know About Us:

What I Promise Her Today:

What I Want Her To Know Today:

I Am Grateful For Her Because:

It's Important To Me That You:

It's Important To Me That We:

What I Need Today:

What I Did For Myself Today:

Today's Goal/s:

What I Want God To Know About Us:

What I Promise Him Today:

What I Want Him To Know Today:

I Am Grateful For Him Because:

It's Important To Me That You:

It's Important To Me That We:

What I Need Today:

What I Did For Myself Today:

Date:

HIS	**HER**
Today's Goal/s:	Today's Goal/s:
What I Want God To Know About Us:	What I Want God To Know About Us:
What I Promise Her Today:	What I Promise Him Today:
What I Want Her To Know Today:	What I Want Him To Know Today:
I Am Grateful For Her Because:	I Am Grateful For Him Because:
It's Important To Me That You:	It's Important To Me That You:
It's Important To Me That We:	It's Important To Me That We:
What I Need Today:	What I Need Today:
What I Did For Myself Today:	What I Did For Myself Today:

Made in the USA
Columbia, SC
07 September 2018